A STORIES

Life Story of a Butterfly

Charlotte Guillain

Chicago, Illinois

© 2015 Heinemann Library
an imprint of Capstone Global Library, LLC
Chicago, Illinois

All rights reserved. No part of this publication may be reproduced or transmitted in any form or by any means, electronic or mechanical, including photocopying, recording, taping, or any information storage and retrieval system, without permission in writing from the publisher.

Edited by Catherine Veitch and Gina Kammer
Designed by Richard Parker and Peggie Carley
Picture research by Mica Brancic
Production by Victoria Fitzgerald
Originated by Capstone Global Library Ltd

Library of Congress Cataloging-in-Publication Data
Cataloging-in-publication information is on file with the Library of Congress.

ISBN 978-1-4846-0487-8 (hardcover)
ISBN 978-1-4846-0492-2 (paperback)
ISBN 978-1-4846-0502-8 (eBook PDF)

Acknowledgments

We would like to thank the following for permission to reproduce photographs:

Alamy: Don Johnston, 9, Eric Carr, 20, Marvin Dembinsky Photo Associates, 12, 28 (right), Survivalphotos, 8, 24, 28 (left); FLPA: Minden Pictures/Ingo Arndt, 19, 22; Getty Images: Kerri Wile, 27, Oxford Scientific/Ed Reschke, cover; Science Source: E. R. Degginger, 7, Eileen Tanson, 11, Phil Degginger, 15, 29 (left), Scott Camazine, 14, Stuart Wilson, 16; Shutterstock: AlexussK (stone design element), cover and throughout, Cathy Keifer, 10, 13, Cynthia Kidwell, 21, 29 (right), Hurst Photo, 23, jannoon028 (grass border), throughout, kingfisher, 17, Leighton Photography & Imaging, 5, Melola, 18, Sari ONeal, 4, wizdata, 6, Yuliya Proskurina (green leaves border), cover and throughout; SuperStock: Minden Pictures, 25, 26

We would like to thank Michael Bright for his assistance in the preparation of this book.

Every effort has been made to contact copyright holders of material reproduced in this book. Any omissions will be rectified in subsequent printings if notice is given to the publisher.

All the Internet addresses (URLs) given in this book were valid at the time of going to press. However, due to the dynamic nature of the Internet, some addresses may have changed, or sites may have changed or ceased to exist since publication. While the author and publisher regret any inconvenience this may cause readers, no responsibility for any such changes can be accepted by either the author or the publisher.

Printed in the United States 5636

Contents

What Is a Butterfly? 4
A Butterfly's Life Story. 6
It Starts with an Egg 8
The Egg Hatches 10
A Growing Caterpillar 12
Changing into a Pupa 14
Changing into an Adult 18
Mating 22
A Butterfly's Life 26
Butterfly Life Story Diagram 28
Glossary 30
Find Out More 31
Index 32

Some words are shown in bold, **like this.** You can find out what they mean by looking in the glossary.

What Is a Butterfly?

A butterfly is a type of animal called an **insect.** Insects are animals with three pairs of legs and a body with three main parts. Many insects have wings.

There are many types of butterflies. They live in many places around the world and can be different sizes and colors.

A Butterfly's Life Story

Like all other animals, a butterfly goes through different stages as it grows into an adult. These stages make up an animal's life story.

Follow the life story of butterflies, and watch them change in unusual ways as they develop and grow.

It Starts with an Egg

A butterfly starts its life as an egg. The egg is oval shaped, tiny, and white.

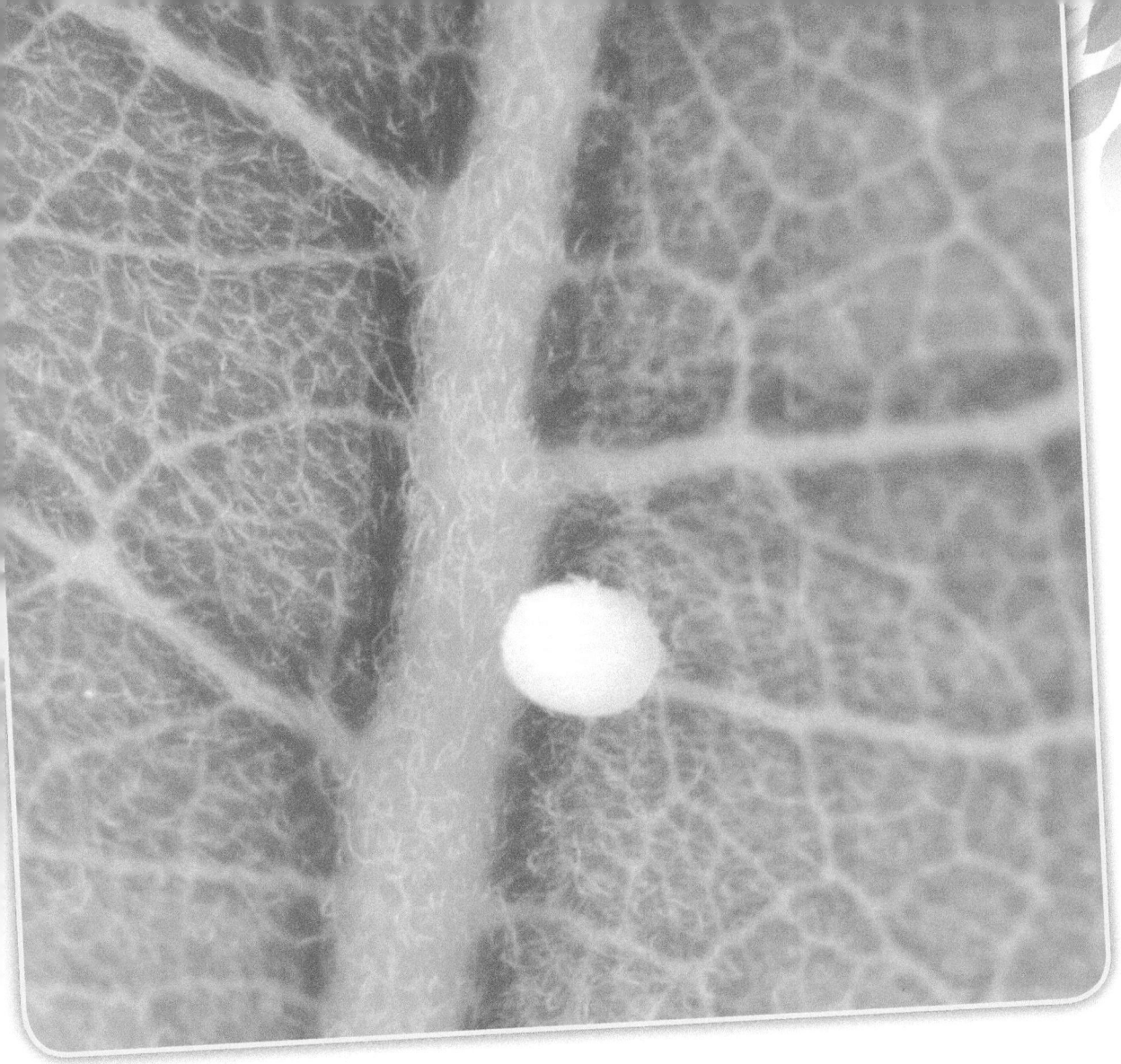

A butterfly's mother usually lays one egg under a leaf. A sticky substance holds the egg onto the plant.

The Egg Hatches

After three to five days the **larva** starts to hatch from the egg.

A butterfly larva is usually called a caterpillar. This tiny caterpillar is pale, with a dark head to start with. As it grows it changes color.

A Growing Caterpillar

The caterpillar starts to eat. First it eats its own egg, and then it starts to feed on the plants around it. It gets bigger and bigger.

The caterpillar grows so much that its skin splits several times. When its skin splits, the caterpillar crawls out with a soft new skin.

Changing into a Pupa

When a caterpillar is very fat, it cannot grow any bigger. It makes a sticky liquid and attaches itself to a twig or leaf.

The caterpillar's skin splits one more time. A **pupa** is now underneath. The pupa has a hard shell. A pupa is sometimes called a **chrysalis.**

The stage when a caterpillar changes into an adult is called a pupa. This change of body shape is called **metamorphosis.**

It takes a monarch butterfly about 10 days to turn into an adult. Other butterflies can take months to change into adults.

Changing into an Adult

When a pupa has changed into an adult butterfly, the shell around it splits open. It slowly comes out of the shell.

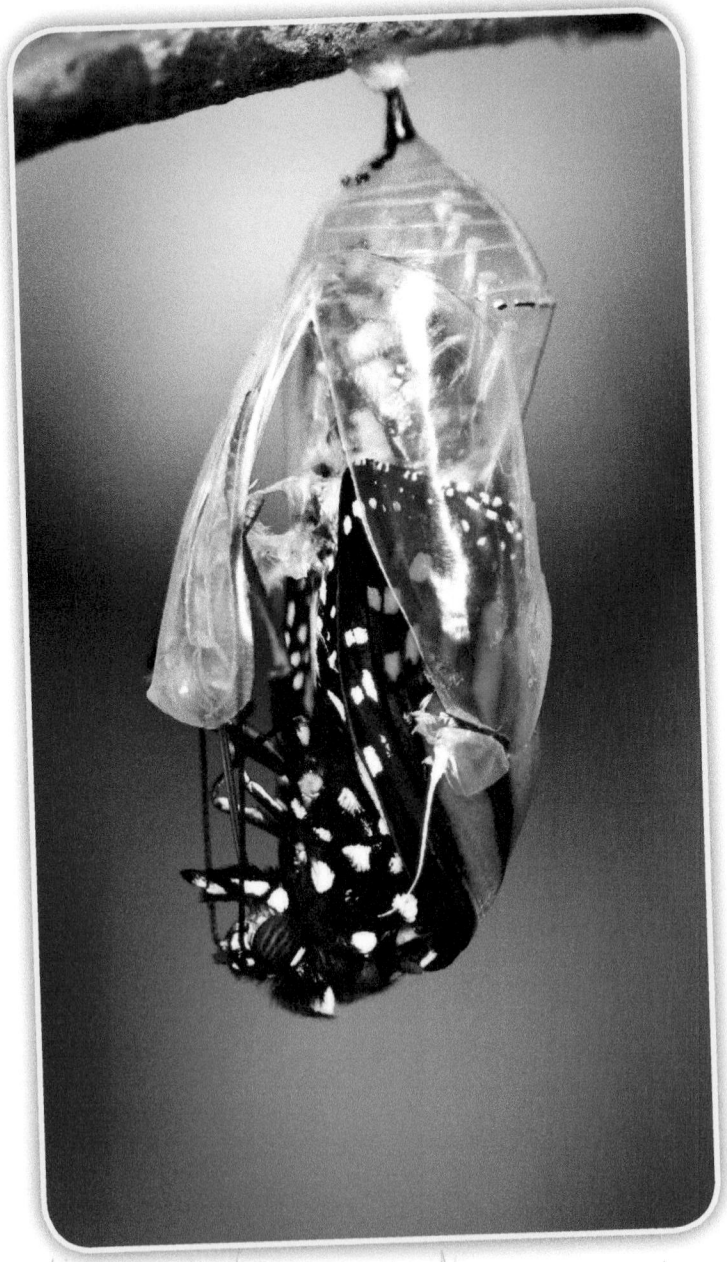

The adult butterfly's wings are soft and damp at first. It has to wait a few hours for its wings to dry and its body to get harder.

Like all insects, an adult butterfly has three body parts. These are the head, the **thorax**, and the **abdomen**.

On a butterfly's head there are two eyes and two **antennae,** which it uses to smell food. In its mouth is a long tube called a **proboscis,** which it uses to suck up food.

Mating

The butterfly looks for a mate, so they can continue the life story. Together they can **reproduce** and create new butterflies.

A female butterfly uses its **antennae** to smell a chemical that a male butterfly makes when it is ready to mate.

After the male and female butterflies have mated, the female is ready to lay eggs. It will usually do this in spring, when the weather is warm.

When a female butterfly has laid eggs on a plant, it leaves them. Sometimes a **predator**, such as an ant, will eat the eggs before they hatch.

A Butterfly's Life

A butterfly cannot live in places that have very cold weather. It flies south to a warmer place to spend the winter.

Most adult butterflies do not live longer than a month. Many butterflies are eaten by predators, such as birds, other insects, and frogs.

Butterfly Life Story Diagram

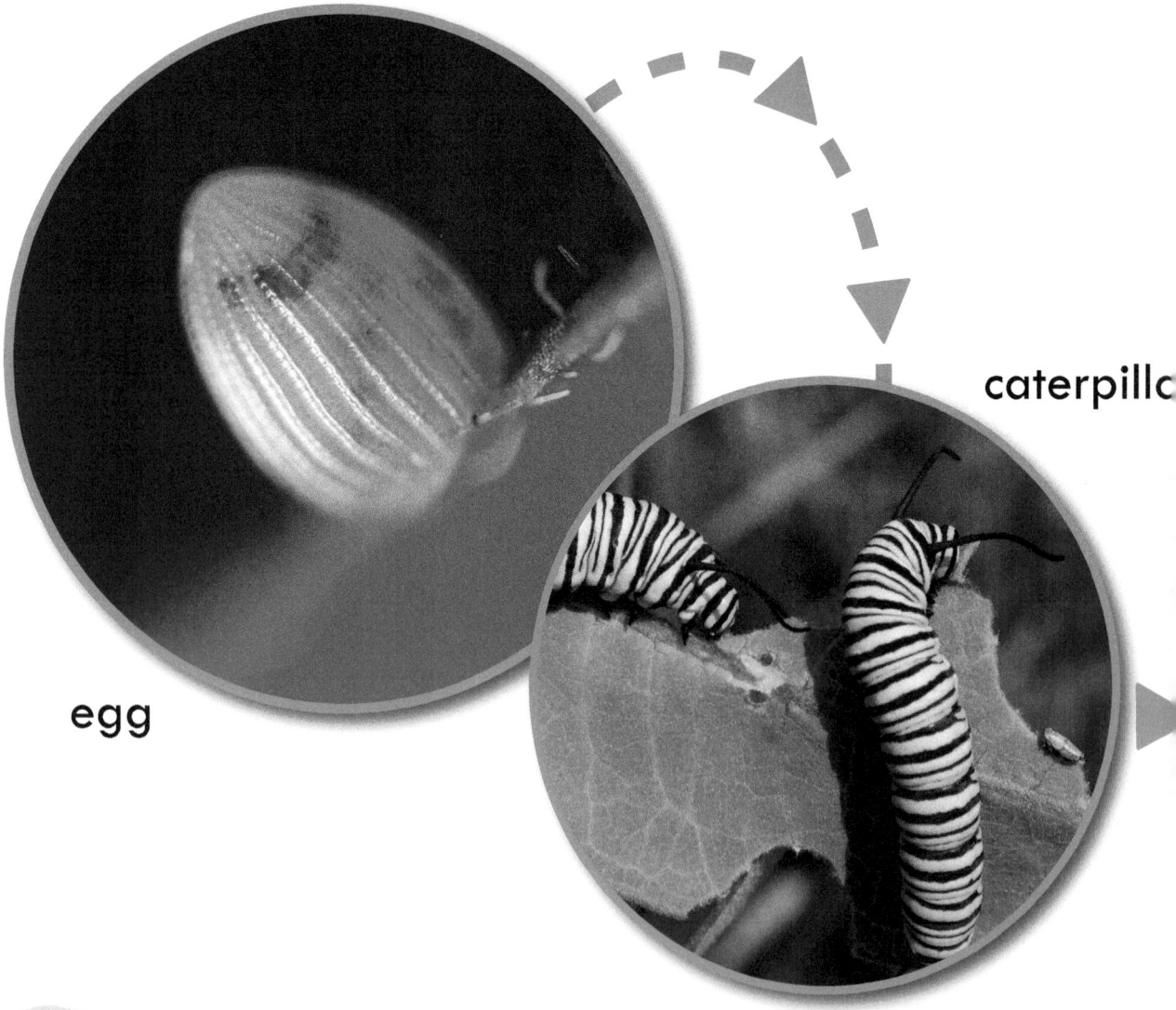

butterfly
chrysalis

Glossary

abdomen lower part of an insect's body, which is joined to the thorax

antennae long, thin feelers on an insect's head that it uses to feel and smell

chrysalis stage of an insect's life when it changes from a larva to an adult; also known as a pupa

insect type of animal with no backbone that has three main body parts and three pairs of legs

larva stage in an animal's life before it becomes an adult

metamorphosis stages where an animal changes body shape and appearance

predator animal that hunts and eats other animals

proboscis long mouthpart, like a tube, that sucks up food

pupa stage of an insect's life when it changes from a larva to an adult

reproduce to lay eggs or give birth to young

thorax part of an insect's body between the head and abdomen

Find Out More

Books

A Monarch Butterfly's Journey, Suzanne Slade
(Picture Window Books, 2012)

Butterflies and Moths, Clare Hibbert
(Arcturus Publishing, 2011)

Sensational Butterflies Sticker Book
(Natural History Museum, 2013)

Websites

http://www.bbc.co.uk/nature/life/Lepidoptera
Visit the BBC Nature website to find out more about butterflies and watch video clips.

http://kids.nationalgeographic.com/kids/animals/creaturefeature/monarch-butterflies/
Visit the National Geographic website to find out about Monarch butterflies.

Index

abdomen 20
adult 6, 16, 17, 18, 19
antennae 21, 23
body 4, 16, 19, 20
caterpillar 11, 12, 13, 14, 16, 28
chrysalis 15, 29
eat 12, 25
egg 8, 9, 10, 12, 24, 25, 28
food 21
habitat 26
head 11, 20, 21
insect 4, 20, 27
larva 10, 11
leaf 9, 14
life span 27
metamorphosis 16
predator 25, 27
proboscis 21, 30
pupa 14, 15, 16, 18
reproduce 22
shell 15, 18
skin 13, 15
smell 21, 23
thorax 20
weather 24, 26
wings 4, 19